Birth of the
Owl Butterflies

Birth of the Owl Butterflies

RUTH SHARMAN

PICADOR

First published 1997 by Picador

an imprint of Macmillan Publishers Ltd
25 Eccleston Place, London SW1W 9NF
and Basingstoke

Associated companies throughout the world

ISBN 0 330 35265 2

1 3 5 7 9 8 6 4 2

A CIP catalogue record for this book is available from
the British Library.

Typeset by SetSystems, Saffron Walden, Essex
Printed and bound in Great Britain by
Mackays of Chatham plc, Chatham, Kent

For my mother and father

Acknowledgements

Many thanks to the editors of the following, in which some of these poems, or versions of them, have appeared: *Sunday Times, Observer, Independent, London Magazine, Poetry Review, Modern Poetry in Translation, The Faber Book of Murder* and the Staple First Editions series (1997).

'Birth of the Owl Butterflies' won second prize in the 1989 Arvon International Poetry Competition, and 'On Seeing' and 'Blade' won prizes in the 1990 National Poetry Competition and the 1994 Canterbury Festival Poetry Competition, respectively.

Contents

I

II

III

I

My Good Coat

It's a coat
for answering back,
for lounging in
and leaving ashtrays
on the arms of chairs,
a coat for when
you're feeling bored
or small and lonely,
a coat that says
this woman calls the shots,
she's sexy, rich, adored;
a coat that cries
for spiky heels
and crimson lips,
a coat whose fur lapel
softly falls around
its owner's throat
and glides towards her toes,
whose silk inside's
the shade of raspberry-
juice and moss,
a coat for committing
some delicious sin,
for wearing loose
with nothing underneath
but skin.

Touch

From the plum tree I could see the sky
and look across the fields that rolled up
to our garden fence and down to where
a curve of trees followed the contours
of the hills and hid a stream

I'd spend hours damming and undamming,
where only water-sounds would break
the stillness or a sudden flash
of wings, and in spring a mass of violets
flowered in the shadows, scented, white.

There were three of us building dams
the day the big boys came and told us
to take off our clothes and *Touch. Go on, touch,*
so we shackled our knees with trouser legs
and touched each other in places

                          we'd not touched before.

They laughed, kicked a stone or two and left . . .
We watched as water seeped at first,
then prised apart all that our hands had done
and the whole muddy torrent came bursting through
with its cargo of leaves and scum.

Conger

He lies there bloated and still
in the shadows:
blue-black fruit
that's ready to burst.

I wonder,
if I dipped my finger in,
would he lunge,
though he's already breakfasted
on dead flesh?

If I wrapped my hands
round his waist
– though they'd never reach –
would he feel like warm velvet
or cold and slick like slime?

Since he's no more
than an eating machine,
would I even know
where his belly began?

We watch
for a flicker of life
from his lightless eyes.
                    Then suddenly
this eel that's she to you
and he to me
shifts like a shadow
beyond our grasp.

Arachnophobia

There seems to be no cure
– not even in knowing
that a Frenchman spun
socks from the silk

or that in Colombia
they're said to piggyback
the souls of the dead
up to heaven;

there can be no truce
with wolf or widow
(her belly bulging
like a Gladstone bag)

or the one that weaves
a subterranean lair
and lines it with silk
and listens at the door,

or even the harvestman
I saw sucking red juices
out of a beetle's back
in a field of alpine flowers.

I imagine bathfuls,
dream them falling
from rafters
in a tumbledown house,

feel their squiggling legs
in the bed, swarming
under night clothes, probing
into eyes, ears, nose,

furring the inside
of my mouth and running down
my throat, so when I call
for my mother

the sound dies
amidst the blackness
of a million million
minute hairs.

Waterlilies

Few things achieve
the immaculate whiteness
of these waterstars

drawn by a child
who thinks of sky-stars
as stemless flowers

and has laid them here
to float among dragonflies
and waterboatmen

on a surface that reflects
trees, leaves and lilies
but gives nothing away

of that other world,
swollen stems reaching down
through darkness to where

spider eggs are hatching,
caddis grubs are building
homes from sticks and stones,

and if you've delved
into that darkness,
you'll know the soft, cold ooze

that sneaks between your toes
as you step in, and how,
as you thrash to free yourself,

those supple roots wrap
insistently around your legs,
slippery as eels.

Cobaea scandens

These pods are time bombs
hanging off our front fence,
in every one a hundred seeds
just waiting to leap out.
People steal them, attracted
by huge flowers opening creamy green,
darkening in days to lilac, purple:
cups on saucers, homely
but beautiful in their way.
What they don't know
is how fast this thing grows: that
you can almost see the tendrils move
as the vine sprawls across the fence,
reaching for handhold after handhold,
then sweeping towards the house.
Leave the window open a crack
and it's in, slithering
across the floor, eager to explore
inside the airing cupboard
and under the fridge,
slipping up the stairs,
feeling its way into the bathroom,
nosing between the sheets.

The House

The plates are itching
to rearrange themselves
in the kitchen cupboard

– and listen to those squeaks
and scratchings
from the cutlery drawer.

The jars on the bathroom shelf
have turned their labels
to the wall and are dreaming

of cocktails – Corsodyl
with ylang ylang and myrrh,
Tuscany, Mycota and lime –

while in the wardrobe
suit trousers are screwing up
their creases, silk dresses

preparing to leap
from the rails and hang-glide
down to the floor.

The red rug is remembering
a hotter place – hibiscus
flowers and dancing girls –

and in the bed something's
starting to get lively
underneath the wedding lace.

Cleopatra's Island

Look how white the sand is and how the water
turns the blue of kingfisher wings, while further
out to sea it deepens against the mountains,
                    turning to midnight.

People say that Antony shipped these sand grains –
each translucent sphere like a polished moonstone –
all the way from African shores, so she'd be
                    walking on whiteness.

In amongst the olives, where wind is snatching
silver light from leaves and the sea's reflections
run like tongues down branches and over broken
                    arches, imagine

tongues and fingers sliding down sun-warmed bodies,
glints of light from flickering lashes, lowered
voices. Then imagine a wife who, after
                    settling his children,

lies awake, tormented, and in the darkness
sees the breasts and thighs he prefers, and sees him
touch them, growing hard for that other woman
                    over and over.

The Ephesian Artemis

She looks fertile enough
to repopulate the earth,
garlanded with grapes,
with lions at her shoulders
and corn-sheaves round her wrists,
the testes of a dozen bulls
sprouting where her breasts should be.

But look at her city now.
Beyond the cypress trees
where once the Kaystros met the sea
the water's turned to dust
and in her faded streets
Medusa heads are gawping at the sky
and gladiators fight the wind.

Though priests bathed in bull's blood
and slashed between their thighs,
still the river silted up,
mosquitoes came, and malaria,
and Ephesus died. And Artemis
just stands there reaching out,
as if she held a tray of sweets.

Blade

Some vegetables resist
more vigorously
than others.

To vary things
she plays at cutting
herringbones and ovals,

teasing the skin
with her point before
penetrating the heart,

pictures a fingertip
nestling among peelings
on the spattered board,

and, for the luxury
of granting him
a reprieve perhaps,

imagines stepping
to where her husband sits
absorbed

and steering the knife
quite casually
into his side,

curious to see
his look of surprise, feel
how smoothly a blade can slide.

Dressing Up

Patent pumps were safe enough,
and popper beads and glitter,
then the 'Cherry Spice'
you smeared around your lips
while bundling socks
inside a makeshift bra;
and, later, velvet loons
and platform soles, the art
of sticking plastic to your eyes
and taking three-hour baths.
But in time you came to know
the risks attached to clothes,
that some resist removal:
those shoes with blades for heels
that seem a living part
of you, or the black basque,
a present from your lover
with serious laces up the back.
If he's unwilling to set you free
you'll find the more you fight
the more it tightens its silk
around your heart.

The Dress

I wandered through a mansion in my dream
where countless dresses hung from countless rails.
Some were made of velvet, some of silk,
chenille or lace, and some were filmy veils
that slipped beneath my fingertips, soft
and shimmering in shades of white and cream.

I chose one and my husband helped me in.
In cut and shape it differed from the rest,
tapering to a mermaid's tail, its neck
revealing curves I lacked in life.
                              The dress
he hooked me into was my wedding dress,
and it was black and fitted like a skin.

The Bride

They always told me I was bad,
so it was a shock
to hear my dad talking
about his lovely daughter
(the lovely child she'd always been).
It was too late now
to hear such praise,
and as he spoke
I put aside my lilies
and unpinned the veil
that floated down my tight-laced back,
then one by one uncoiled
each strand of hair
from the heavy mass around my head.
My father raised his glass;
the guests raised theirs,
and as they gazed at me
what they saw were hissing snakes
and what I saw was stone.

Mummy

Dearest, we'll start by removing
the bits you won't need any more

– just a delicate cut –
before bathing you inside and out;

then we'll sweeten your flesh
with cinnamon, cedar and myrrh.

So you shine like a god, we'll wrap leaves
of electrum round fingers and toes,

and those muscular shoulders and legs
we'll keep toned

by secreting soft shavings of *Ficus*
just under the skin.

We'll salt you in crystals of natron
and bathe you again.

Then we'll bind. Do it finger
by finger,

and strap down those hands that have strayed,
in a cross at your heart.

With your torso and limbs
we'll arrange a neat parcel in lattice designs

while reserving the narrowest bands
for your head,

which we'll wrap from the left,
then the right, the same number of times,

gently sealing those lips that have lied
with the linen's soft kiss.

Once you're upright,
I'll breathe in your mouth

and I'll open your eyes
to a world in which nothing has changed.

All around will be things that you know.
You'll have garlands, and honey with milk,

while that niche by the door
will be perfectly placed

for watching me come
and then go.

Cookery Lesson

Look for a cap of greenish tan
veined with darker threads
and expanding as it opens,
a stem with a bulbous base
and (crucially) a double ring
connected loosely by a sheath.

You may have to probe to find
the lower part inside the soil
(you should be wearing gloves).
Bear in mind it has no smell
(or taste) and that its flesh
won't darken in the light

or blacken a silver spoon –
these are old wives' tales –
and that it peels as easily
as the sort you buy off shelves
while no amount of cooking
can destroy its qualities.

A tiny piece will be enough
for an entire casserole or pie,
but be patient: *Amanita*'s slow
to work its magic, needing hours
to disperse its flavour
round the bloodstream;

but by the time it's reached
liver, kidneys, heart and spleen
there'll be nothing left to pump
and little hope of help
from cider vinegar and honey
or *cervelles de lapin* soup . . .

Fury

I'm going to bag up
the man who yelled 'Bitch'
from a passing car

with uncles who say
they don't lay down the law
but do, friends who trade

in spiteful truths,
that specialist too special
to talk things through . . .

and I'm going to give
the bag a good shake
until each marble-head

I never had the chance
to answer back
knocks against the next

with a crystalline crack;
then I'll tip them out
on the kitchen floor

and send them tumbling
under the fridge,
to lie among the piles

of dust and broken pills
where silverfish
are looking for lunch.

The White Garden

I'm going to rip out the iceberg roses,
the rocket whose sweetness,
after dark, attracts the moths,
the Madonna lilies and myrtle
and pale bleeding hearts;
inject the heat of marigolds
and blowsy orange poppies
and plant that rose as black
as a woman's blood before it flows.
I'll call a truce with aphids
and the choking fronds of creepers,
stop cutting back the nettles
and cleaning out the pond.
I'll let the sycamore saplings grow
until they're giants against the sun,
and leeches breed in damp places
among the leaves, and snakes thick
as a man's arm infest the trees.
There'll be no peace: the air
will be full of rustlings and cries.
And in the twilight of the underforest
I'll be there, waiting for you
with my pipe and poison darts.

II

Berceuse

Hush! You're getting closer all the time.
You're warm. Death doesn't dawdle or leave the path:
if he's close to the first word of the first line,
he'll be closer still when you get to the last.

Don't imagine he'll saunter off to sleep
among the trees, or pause for breath while you write.
Even as you drink from that mouth whose sweet
moisture slakes the deepest thirst, whose cries

are soft; even as you tighten the knot your four
arms have tied to brace and steady you both
in the burning darkness of her hair and yours –

who knows by what buried trails and hidden detours
he's coming towards you both – hush! – with every
word you write and every breath you draw.

(*after* Philippe Jaccottet)

Dusk

and as he spoke
it was as if I heard the larks
and saw the drifts of whiteness
weighing down the hawthorn trees
and smelt their musk
and felt the wind pursuing
shadows over hills and fields

and as he turned to me
I remembered
the lines that fanned out
from the corners of his eyes
like traces the sea leaves
on the sand, and how
their colour shifted like the sea's

and I hesitated
uncertain, dismayed

but already a sweet heaviness
weighed down my lids
already his face was blurring
and the familiar voice
began to fade

and though I would once
have gone with him anywhere
I let him walk towards the light
and did not follow

and the world of whiteness and change
where summer was always
a promise or a memory
dispersed in the indifferent air

The Glass Hall

(Bodrum Museum, Turkey)

Against the darkness
the colours shift from purple
through to blue and green
like light refracted
from a *Morpho*'s wings
or layers shuffled by the sea.

A twisted rod is sunshine
filtering through willow leaves,
while time has forested with ferns
and mapped with continents
these vials once filled
with sandalwood and rose

and used by women wearing
bracelets such as these;
and here are swans' necks
and flasks the shape of udders,
a lid whose nipple is sucking
on the deepest liquid blue,

beakers where lions pad
on leaf-like feet,
supple-backed as scorpions –
and all these pale transparencies
floating in the darkened hall,
like stars seeding

the blackness of space,
were blown from the same blackness
as this Syrian ingot
around whose massive base
a rim of midnight sea
still burns and burns.

Waking in a Strange Room

It's as if a dome of glass were perched
above the city, and high up there
the swifts were searching for an exit,
their cries defining the fixity of space –

the way that slab of morning sunlight
on the floor defines the heat outdoors,
while through the window red geraniums
and terracotta roofs are making statements

about density and weight, a metal disc
is communicating with the nearest star
and a linden tree sends waves of scent
through a hundred feet of air;

though hours ago that tree was just a patch
of night, those houses shoeboxes set on end
and furnished by a child, with matchboxes
for tables, cotton reels for chairs.

The Hold

For weeks we've been moving things,
looking for a favourite book or tape,
a place where each of us could escape
and stow our separate belongings;

now, slowly, while you're away
I wander through these rooms tonight
in darkness mixed with streetlight
and watch the plant-shadows play,

take in the curve of a chair, the line
of a cupboard, the scalloped ring
of a plate, as if seeing each thing
for the first time –

seeing the patterns they create
in the half-light, the way
shapes blur and sway,
lines and curves interrelate –

and as one by one each house light
goes out, our first home starts quietly
drawing away from the quay,
moving off into the night.

Rain

The morning slows to the sound
of your breathing, and the sound
of the rain that is loosening
the last of the winter leaves;
and as the world of solid things
recedes, we're floating in water,
hearing the swishing of cars
or a blackbird's sudden alarm
filtered through distance, unreal,
fooling ourselves that we're safe
and time has no place here, as if
these were the walls of an ark –
not a walnut shell, set afloat
by a child, racing past the kerb
towards those gaps in the grating.

Almost Summer

On days like this
words must be light and fast
to catch the way
the wind brushes over the meadows
turning grass to silver

or describe
the different densities of white
from Sweet Cicely to May

and how a web of larksong
hangs in the sky
glistening with rain

while higher still
a glider drifts, remote,
its wings flashing in sunlight,
then tilts to a darker stroke
against the grey
and dives from sight.

The Funeral

They'd tried to tidy away the mud
behind fake-grass mats
that masked the fresh-cut walls
a digger's blade had seamed:
hung like the antimacassars
she'd sewn with cottage flowers.

But the stuff got everywhere
the day they buried my aunt.
It oozed between the planks
bridging gravel path and grave,
engulfing the mourners' shoes
in a richly creaming tide.

We straggled round, migrant birds
stranded on our separate isles,
as they fought to ease her down.
My young cousin stood closest,
draped in his outsize coat,
clutching a posy of primroses.

At the mention of dust and ash,
he stepped to the edge
and threw his flowers down.
I imagined them in the half-light,
their pale skin bruised
by the first crush of mud to come.

Making Jam

It was magic of a sort, the way
she let the drops of syrup fall, to form
those solid jewels on her setting plate
while night closed in around the kitchen's warmth.

The ripe fruit spread its sweetness through the house
and as she stirred, the purple darkness turned
to deepest rose that seethed and frothed white, round
the edges of her pan, and slowly firmed.

She'd make as much as twenty pots at once
in better years. We find the odd jar still
tucked in behind the packet soups and tins
on shelves that home-made things of hers once filled.

And as the written labels slowly blur,
her dark preserves grow layers of bone-white fur.

Hunger

Sometimes only bread will do:
warm loaves
torn open to expose
their soft insides –
bending low, you breathe
their silky sweetness,
dig deep, like a cat,
with eyes half closed,
kneading its memory of milk.

Yellow

It's crocuses
clamouring for the sun

like a nestful
of blackbird beaks

pussy willow
pollen-furred

lemons and pudding wine
a last freckling of leaves

lightening the darkness
of sycamore trees

paper spotted by time
and milk gone sour

something leaked
onto hospital white

and my mother's face
turned into her pillow

small and tight
and beaked like a bird's

White-Out

Flame trees flowered
around the garden walls –
flames before the leaves –

and on the pond
waterlilies opened,
crimson, after dark;

and on nights too hot
for pillows we'd swim
under the Gymkhana lights,

eat chips in chilli sauce
and sleep on the roof
to catch the breeze.

And even if poisonous
red centipedes lived
inside the potting shed

and a cobra took
my white dove, even if
people who had no hands

and only half a face
came begging at the gate,
I was used to these.

At five I left behind
one mother who'd held me
through the monsoon nights

and sailed across an ocean
with the other,
to a washed-out place

where there were clocks,
blazers, shoelaces and ties,
knives and no curry,

a garden full of nettles,
a house whose roof of straw
let in the rain;

and a day came
when a whiteness stole
the shadows from the trees,

rubbed out colours,
stopped the sounds
and swallowed up the sky.

The Walled Garden

My mother had trouble with words.
I doubt she'd have known 'metastasise'
until her illness spilled and spread:
a tongue-twister to add to her confusion.
Flustered by clever company she'd mispronounce
the easiest ones: forget, say, the soft g
in *rouge*, and later glow with shame.

Hers was a vocabulary of growing things.
Hooped Petticoats and Peeping Toms
were daffodils she loved for their dainty names,
and even Latin came easily when applied
to those lilies of the haziest blue
or the shrub that blazed by the garden wall
and needed shielding from the frost.

She preferred a wilderness to a park,
encouraging leaves to spill, coaxing
our tiny garden to year-round disarray.
And when a cool oasis greened between
our limestone walls, took refuge in its shade:
protecting her complexion from those clusters
that budded deep inside her when they came.

On Seeing

(Monet's Series Paintings)

We fixed the blueprint long ago, and see
our way through life by well-worn marks and signs,
half-registering trees and skies, the lines
that shape a face we've filed in memory.

While he sees hayricks fired by day's first light,
those pearly ice floes, oatfields, poplars warmed
through rose to gold and rust which, losing form,
go drifting back to greyness, mist and night,

I'm surprised how every autumn gathers pace
and dull to subtle shifts, the minor keys:
while seeing drama in the dying leaves,
I missed the dying in my mother's face.

Out There

This was you in the early days
wearing that wide blue skirt
and your camera smile,
cream-skinned despite the heat.

You'd sailed the length of Suez.
Seen shoals of silver fish in flight
and the flame trees' leafless
branches catching light.

You'd crossed Himalayan passes
through iris and poppy fields,
picknicked on white beaches
and summered in the hills;

worn marigold garlands, fingered
fruit shaped like hearts and stars
while lepers groped for handouts
and small birds sang behind bars.

You'd learnt to kill your time
taking tea at the Gymkhana pool
and later cocktails, relinquishing
your children to the rules;

letting others fix the backdrop
of your day, sweep the paths,
make the beds, mop our faces,
cook the meals, drive the cars.

And already forty years ago
you had that frown around your eyes
as you looked back past the camera
to a different life, one more your size.

Inventory

I've inherited ten identical lipsticks
(such things keep coming to light),
Revlon 'Pink Vanilla', grainy with age,
each one rounded down to inch-height;

a handkerchief in delicate linen,
its label still hand-stitched in place –
4 Rupees, Infant Jesus Orphanage,
Mulagumoodu, genuine South Indian lace;

that clumsy tapestry, come full circle,
one of my half-remembered gifts
you'd stored in your special drawer,
with its frame now half adrift;

and a diary with its pages blank,
except for PERM, vigorously underlined
in time for your birthday, your second
to last: October seventy-nine.

Ghost

She comes to me at night,
but keeps her distance,
moving silently in lighted rooms
the other side of glass.

My father bought me this sober little book
when I was still too young to comprehend
the reproductive processes in flowers,
its talk of ovules, perianths and angiosperms.

The plates showed in black and white a hundred
varieties of grass, and puzzled us with *Compositae*
and Umbellifers that were hard to tell apart,
so we played a game of 'Spot the Difference'.

After each walk I'd colour in another vetch or daisy,
blurring the edges like an old lady's lipstick,
adding 'Nobottle Woods' or 'Wadenhoe Marsh'
in writing that joined up with the years.

The book was a way of talking to my dad
(who always did talk best through things)
and as I look at the crinkled creamy pages,
at all the blank spaces among the brightness,

I want to see those missing flowers filled in
and write the names for places we never knew
until every page is thick with ink and pastel
and what was left unsaid is said in silence now.

Birth of the Owl Butterflies

They hung in our kitchen for days:
a row of brown lanterns that threw no light,
merely darkened with their growing load.
Pinned to a shelf among the knick-knacks
and the cookery books;
ripening in the radiator's heat:
six Central American *Caligo* chrysalids,
five thousand miles from their mountain home.

My father had brought them here,
carefully packed in cotton wool,
to hatch, set, identify, and display:
these unpromising dingy shells plumped up
like curled leaves, on each a silver spur,
a tiny gleam or drop of dew,
Nature had added as a finishing touch
to perfect mimicry.

For weeks the wizened fruit had been maturing.
Now, one by one, the pods exploded,
crackling in the quiet kitchen,
and a furry missile emerged – quickly,
as if desperate to break free –
unhinged its awkward legs,
hauling behind it, like a frilly party dress,
the rumpled mass of its soft wings.

It clung unsteadily to the cloven pod,
while slow wings billowed with the blood
that pumped them full.
The dark velvet began to glow
with a thousand tiny striations,
and there, in each corner,
boldly ringed in black and gold,
two fierce owl-eyes widened.

Uneasy minutes, these, before *Caligo*
can flex its nine-inch wings and fly.
They drooped still, gathering strength,
limp flags loosely flowing.
When two butterflies hatched too close,
and clashed, each scrabbling for a footing,
one fell and its wings flopped
fatly on the kitchen floor.

I pictured them shattering later
on taps and cupboard corners;
but my father gauged his moment well,
allowed a first few timid forays,
then swooped down gentle-fingered
with his glass jar for the kill.
The monstrous wings all but filled it,
beat vigorously, fluttered, and were still.

Grayling, Gatekeeper,
Comma, Ringlet, Marbled White
and Meadow Brown,
the Queen of Spain
and all her English relatives . . .
I have a store of names
that make me think of you

and all those August afternoons
I've trailed behind you
through some wilderness
of wood or marsh or scrub,
the hours (it seemed) I'd sit and wait
while you ploughed on ahead,
and then complain.

And now I'm adding to the list
as we stand waist deep in brambles
watching for a flash
of orange in the wind,
then scramble up a rocky combe
looking down to Lynmouth
and to Wales across the water;

and when I ask you
why a Green Fritillary
with just three weeks to fly
should choose this windy hillside
high above the sea,
your answer makes me glad
to be my father's daughter.

Blues

Most of us can simply say
that it's a butterfly,
and that it's small and blue

but you see a border,
a certain arrangement of dots,
the faintest shift towards silver

or turquoise . . . and, even on the wing,
can tell the Chalk-Hill
from the Holly or the Common Blue.

You'd like to find Adonis
but we've missed his brief season
by a week or two and you decide

there are fewer Marbled Whites,
fewer Peacocks, Painted Ladies
since last time you were here

(though to me the whole hillside
seems alive with wings), fewer
harebells and trefoil.

We're walking on earthworks
on a day so clear that from up here
we can look across four counties

and out across the hills which men
whose bones lie buried in this chalk
once scanned for fires,

who saw forests where we see fields,
but the same convergence of sea and sky
in that ambiguous band of blue.

But you're focussing on butterflies,
not the view, and I'm content to follow
and look for what you want to find,

surprised how easily I catch
a tiny Hairstreak and hold it
for a moment in my hand.

In the Glasshouse with my Father

As if your skin
were weeping sugar tears
that hardened in the sun,
these crusty white secretions

keep appearing on your hands,
and now your cheek,
a legacy of Indian skies
you can't afford to keep.

And because you've torn
some tissue deep inside,
and it won't heal
(another telltale sign),

we walk more slowly
than last time we were here,
relishing this atmosphere
that's hard to breathe,

pushing through the heat,
searching for the tree
that grew beside our house
with iris flowers

and leaves like camels' feet,
swept back thirty years
by the force of one sweet scent
whose source we fail to trace.

And you're amazed
when I can name this lily
that grew wild in the woods
(whose fruit were used for beads),

unaware that gods inhabited
the space beneath the garden seat
and to placate them
I left offerings there –

flowerheads and the *Gloriosa*'s
glossy black-red seeds,
as a bowerbird arranges
treasures to attract a mate.

Two Robins

She needs testosterone
if she's to sing,
so leaves the music
to her mate,

that plump ventriloquist
who likes to decorate
our Buddha's head
with blobs of white

while she's preoccupied
with food, preparing
for the weeks to come,
and eats for six or eight

and in the interims
sorts through leaves,
selecting this, rejecting that
for reasons of her own.

Each has a role to play:
these things are simple.
But what if he can't make
the notes? And what if

having built a home,
she tries to lay an egg
but finds that every shell
decides to break?

Tides

Or, put it another way:

imagine an ocean
where banks of coral bloom
and fragile forests sway
in the ocean swell,

where ghostly creatures float
through trees
reflecting the light,
and soft mouths open and close;

then think of a net
as it snags and tightens,
cradling a weight of sour water
and not a single fish.

Perfume Bottle

This pink-veined minaret,
inverted teardrop,
tapers down to stand in a pool
of rainbow light with, snaking round,
a rope of woven thread which swells
to form an oval bulb
that fits inside my hand,
while dimly through the glass
a whitish tube curls, ghostly,
like an embryo, to sip
the warm, sweet residue.

Unborn

When I dream of her
she changes shape,
shrinks to kitten size
or flows like water
over outstretched hands.
And even when the stream
becomes a baby I can hold
– a daughter of my own,
wrapped inside a quilt
as warm and soft
as kitten fur –
my baby looks at me
with lifeless eyes
and when I touch her skin
it feels as cold as stone.

Rumpelstiltskin

I'll wash my hands seven times
after touching meat
and talk in whispers

I'll wear a hat out walking,
repress the urge
to fondle dogs and cats

I'll eat the brightest greens
and drink the sweet white milk
of mountain goats

I'll learn to sing for her
and play her simple tunes
on her father's flute

I'll sleep when *she* decides
and move so softly
she'll not feel a thing in there

– but if the bogeyman comes
and claims her as his own
what magic can I do

to counter his
when he could answer to
a million different names?

Night-Light

Cradled in my arms,
she makes the shape
of one of those leafboats
with a cargo of candles and flowers
set to float on the Ganges at dusk.

She shudders in the dream-current
that shakes her sides,
then sleeps on, face flushed
with roses, her small flame
glowing in the dark.